NORWAY

SWEDEN

FINLAND

RUSSIA

TRÆNA

RØDØY

POLCIRKELN

JOKKMOKK

ROVANIEMI

POSIO

OLD UMBA & KUZREKA

SALEKHARD & LABYTNANGI

YAMAL & YAR'SALE

ZHIGANSK

66° 33' 44" N

LIFE ON THE LINE CRISTIAN BARNETT
PEOPLE OF THE ARCTIC CIRCLE

Thanks for your support Craig!

C Barnett.

LIFE ON THE LINE CRISTIAN BARNETT

Edited by **HUW LEWIS-JONES**

polarworld

First published in the United Kingdom in 2014 by Polarworld.

www.polarworld.co.uk

Published in France in 2014 by Éditions Paulsen.

Photography © Cristian Barnett
Text © Huw Lewis-Jones, Hugh Brody and Ginny Alexander
Volume © Polarworld

A CIP catalogue record of this book is available from the British Library.

Direction by Huw Lewis-Jones
Designed by Liz House

ISBN 978-0-9555255-8-2

Printed and bound in China by Everbest

For more information about Cristian Barnett, visit www.crisbarnett.com

polarworld

oneocean
EXPEDITIONS

ARCTIC KINGDOM

Paulsen

Cover: **Lars,** Jokkmokk

Page 2: **Nenet Children,** Yamal

Page 4: **Sigurður,** Grímsey
Page 5: **Lyuba**, Knjazaja Guba

Page 6: **Vild-Hasse,** Jokkmokk
Page 7: **Tatyana**, Zhigansk

Page 8: **Evano,** Repulse Bay
Page 9: **Vladimir,** Zhigansk

Page 20-21: **Rest,** Repulse Bay

Page 23: **Waiting,** Kotzebue

Page 180-181: **Camp,** Yamal

Page 200-201: **High-Rise,** Sisimiut

Pius, Repulse Bay

ALASKACANADAGREENLANDICELA

ONORWAY SWEDEN FINLAND RUSSIA

CAPTURING LIGHT

Hugh Brody

To know and then to control the world, geographers and explorers have created all kinds of grids to divide up and measure its surface. Invisible lines wrap around the world to make journeys navigable and descriptions specific. Latitude and longitude are the organisational net in which the globe is caught; degrees of distance between and among these lines make it possible to say where any place can be found, or locate any spot on the earth's surface where you might wish to go.

The line that goes round the middle of the world, the equator, is not quite arbitrary: everything has to have its centre, its division into two halves. The Tropics of Capricorn and of Cancer are a mix of human concerns and natural realities: they mark the degree of latitude where the sun is directly overhead at noon on midsummer's day – 21 June for the northern latitudes, where the Tropic of Cancer marks the line around the earth where the sun thus stands at its highest; 21 December is the day that defines the Tropic of Capricorn, in the southern latitudes. And then there is the Arctic Circle. This is the line where each year there is one day when the sun does not set, and one day when the sun does not rise. A line to show where every midsummer there is an evening of bewitching magic as the sun skirts the horizon, seems to pause, and then, in a refusal of twilight, begins to rise. And where every midwinter there is a night that never brightens into more than the edge of dawn.

In northern Scandinavia that midsummer night on the Arctic Circle is a time of magic and wild ceremony; for the Inuit in the Canadian Far North it is just the longest of many long summer nights, or the shortest of many short winter days. But for many peoples who live far to the south of it, the Arctic Circle is both the epitome of the North and the gateway to it: to cross that imaginary line is to have achieved something, to have reached a region of adventure. So it is both a real place, where something very remarkable happens, and a place of the imagination, an idea about a particular edge of the world – cold, remote, difficult to get to, romantic, perhaps magical. Trolls are given homes up there, Santa and his elves are at work nearby, and it may be a landscape where only the Inuit – with their dog teams and snow-houses – can feel at home.

Cristian Barnett was born and grew up in Newcastle – in the north of England, far from the Arctic Circle. He became a photographer thanks to a rather uninspiring geography teacher, whose 'boring' lessons (so Cristian says) made him dream for a life further afield. He spent most of his time gazing through the window at the nearby art faculty. A kind uncle then encouraged his artistic dreams with a camera and taught him how to process his film. He studied photography for four years and worked for six as a freelance assistant; a ten-year training and apprenticeship during which he discovered all the usual sectors of the profession: shooting products, cars, corporate jobs, advertising and fashion. Establishing himself in his own right, he has won the highest possible reputation as a photographer of food, creating the fabulous, mouth-watering illustrations for books by cookery-writers who include the great Michel Roux Jnr. He has also done elegant portraiture, including *The Alchemy of Wisdom*, a book of astonishingly beautiful images commissioned by the Kuwaiti royal family to celebrate the great minds of their country.

So, the Arctic Circle may seem a long way from the interests and skills that are linked to Cristian Barnett's career as a photographer. But he loved to travel. As a very young man he spent time in Israel and found himself

Timo, Posio

15

Arctic Circle, Rovaniemi

visiting the homes and villages of the Druze, Christian Arabs who live along the borders between Israel, Lebanon and Syria. He then made journeys into other countries of the Middle East – Jordan, Syria, Egypt. This was not travel in order to take photographs. On the contrary, Cristian Barnett is a strong advocate against the camera: for him, it is possible to explore and look and appreciate what you see, or to take photographs. He believes that the two things tend to exclude one another. To travel with the camera in hand is to be looking at the world in order find photographs, not in order to see it. When the great marvels are there in front of you, he says, forget the camera and use the mind.

He remembers being at the calving grounds of the great icebergs as they fracture and fall from the vast Greenlandic glaciers – one of the most awe-inspiring sights, and indeed sounds, in the Arctic. He stood with a group of tourists as close as they dared to the immense drama of a glacier breaking and an iceberg, the size and weight of a twenty-storey hotel, smashing into the sea. He had never experienced anything like it, had never imagined he would come so close to a natural event with such astounding, unfathomable scale and force. He realised, as he watched, that he was the only person not taking photographs: everyone else had a camera between themselves and what they saw. He suspects that he was the only person actually really looking at what was happening in front of them. He is, he says, 'a great believer in not letting photography dominate your experience of life'. And he has gone so far as to acquire a website of the name *www.nophotographyday.com* which, he hopes, one day might be the inspiration for an annual celebration of *not* taking photographs.

A Finnish friend, whom he had met when travelling in the Middle East, one day pointed out where the Arctic Circle ran through Finland. The Arctic Circle – where else did it go? They were on a plane in the sunshine high above the clouds. Cristian Barnett pulled out an inflight magazine and followed its course. It cuts across the north of Finland, then the north of Sweden and about half way up Norway; then over the Norwegian Sea and just past the northern tips of Iceland; then over southern Greenland and across Davis Strait to Canada's Baffin Island; across the two thousand miles of Canadian northern tundra, and then across northern Alaska; over the

Arctic Circle, Polcirkeln

Chukchi Sea and into far eastern Russia; across the Siberian taiga, to the Kola Peninsula and to the Russian Finland border.

For huge distances the Arctic Circle runs over lands where long, icy winters and cool summers mean that trees do not grow more than a few inches above the ground, but where mosses and lichens, alpine plants and dense, tough sedges cover an open land. But in other stretches the invisible line moves through boreal forests and taiga with their vast expanses of tees – pine, hemlock, birch, willow. Across the Canadian tundra the line also goes through thousands of shallow lakes, their water in summer and ice in winter sitting on the permafrost that binds all the subsurface, no more than a metre down, into a solid block of frozen soils. Across Alaska the line goes over a mountain range; through Siberia there are immense stretches of rolling forest and river valleys. The different geographies have different populations of plants, insects, birds and animals. Everywhere there is life, making its adjustment to a terrain where each year there is a day of continuous sunlight, and one night that leads, without a sunrise, to the next.

For each part of the geography there are peoples. Sami, with their reindeer herds in Norway, Sweden and the Kola Peninsula; and the Russian and Scandinavian settlers, with their farms and fishing boats in all these places; the Greenlanders – Inuit and Danes; the Inuit in their communities across the eastern and central Canadian Arctic, the Athabascan First Nations and Inuvialuit in the west Canadian Arctic, where mining, oil and gas and the search for diamonds are bringing another flow of people to the North; and then Athabascans and Inupiak of Alaska. The twelve distinct indigenous peoples of the Russian far east and far north, with Russian developments reaching to and beyond the Arctic Circle – roads, oil and gas developments, even cities, where Russians outnumber what the Soviet regimes labelled as 'the small peoples of the north'.

There is a great deal that can be said about the peoples who live along the Arctic Circle. It makes a link across an immense range of societies, each with its distinctive genius for living in a northern setting. Reindeer herders, moving their flocks between a set of seasonal pastures, have occupied much of Scandinavia and many parts of Siberia, with culture after

culture having evolved patterns of movement for themselves and their herds, over many millennia. The Sami of Finland, Sweden and Norway are well known. But they are one of many such cultures – the Nenets, Ghanzi, Nantsi, Yakut, Eveni, Tungusik and Chuckchi are all reindeer herding and hunting peoples who live on and near the Arctic Circle. As well as herders, there are hunter-gatherers – the speakers of Eskimoan languages – Yuit in Siberia, then the Yupik, Alupiak, Iunvialuit in Alaska, and the Inuit in Canada and Greenland. Also the speakers of Athabascan languages – a whole set of hunters, trappers, fishermen and gatherers whose societies reach across interior Alaska and the forested areas of the Canadian North. The Arctic Circle passes through all of them. And the differences in history, origin and heritage of these peoples is reflected in the differences between the way they speak – Sami, Siberian, Eskimoan and Athabascan languages are as different from one another as English, Hungarian, Mandarin and Japanese. They come from different language families, with quite separate origins and journeys through many thousands of years of distinct linguistic evolution.

The modern complexities of life for many of these peoples come from their experience of newcomers. To travel the Arctic Circle is to make an exploration of northern colonial history. The populations along the line are a result of modern transformations as well as ancient traditions. Even in the harshest of the landscapes, far above the tree line in Arctic Canada or at the easternmost tip of the Chukotsk Peninsula where the remotest corners of Asia and North America are no more than forty miles apart, southern and colonial interests have impinged upon indigenous peoples. In central Siberia and northern Finland there are urban and industrial developments right on the Arctic Circle, and areas where indigenous society has been marginalised or even displaced.

The chance conversation with the friend from Finland caused Cristian Barnett to look at the Arctic Circle and wonder what it might mean to travel to many different points along it. This line around the top of the globe enticed the traveller in him and of course appealed to the photographer. He began to wonder what he might find if he made a series of journeys to the Arctic Circle, choosing the places to go by virtue of these being the ones that it was not impossible to reach using ordinary means of travel. He did not seek to mount some complex and daunting expedition across inaccessible terrain; rather, fascination came from the thought that there were communities of people along this imaginary line for whom this was their home, but between which communities there was not necessarily anything in common – other than an abstraction of geographical reckoning. So he searched along the line for possible destinations, and resolved that he would consider any place that was within thirty-five miles of the line would qualify as 'on' the Arctic Circle.

This led to thirteen trips to the North. Each place Cristian visited was a challenge – not so much of environment, though photography in the Far North is complicated when temperatures drop far below zero, but because each place was very much its own world – and he had the challenge of becoming acquainted with that world, making connections with some of the people there, and capturing it in those fragments of a second and flashes of light that are photographs.

Sometimes he travelled alone. Other times he made these journeys with his friend and editor, the polar author Huw Lewis-Jones, a kindred spirit for beguiling adventures such as this. Sometimes they'd venture along with the help of local guides or people they met who quickly became intrigued by the endeavour. And at all times he and his companions would place themselves in the hands of the communities they reached and in this way their experiences, their journeys, would evolve as they went. This is an exploration of sorts: to journey with open eyes and not too much a sense of modern itineraries to restrict the ride. To be *curious*. To travel to experience each day, to embrace the chance encounters and relish the unlooked for but memorable meetings. That is the heart of it.

Cristian wanted to come away from each place along the Arctic Circle where he had alighted with images that are direct visual messages – nothing so simple or unconsidered or random as a snapshot, but images that have a sense of ease and, where possible, a message of welcome. He hoped to show the warmth that can be found here, contrary perhaps to people's expectations of what the Arctic, or northern Russia in particular, might be. This is a wonderful premise, but a demanding objective too:

in each place he had to find the welcome, an ease about his presence, a sharing in the fascination for the project, and then capture it.

It is here that Cristian Barnett's wise scepticism about photography, or about the extent to which the use of a camera can be a way of not quite paying attention, intersects with this project. He does not go to a sequence of extraordinary landscapes and societies and create a gallery of fine surface images; he does not seek to capture all the appearances of geography or of people. Rather, he brings to us his way of having a conversation with place, and of allowing the people in that place to send their messages through his lens, into this book. He has called this set of images an environmental portraiture.

Cristian has used a favourite Hasselblad camera, an 80mm fixed lens and Kodak colour film for each one of his Arctic portraits, ever since this project began in 2006. It was the end of the film era – he has noted that the technology he was using had remained more or less unchanged since the 1950s. By the time he had begun to prepare the images from the Arctic Circle for his book, that kind of film was no longer available and it was lucky he had bought up a stock of the film so he could complete it. A revolution had taken place – a set of technological transformations – that in the history of photography has a parallel only with the inventions of the 1850s when the very possibility of taking photographs was discovered. This was the last major project that Cristian did before all his equipment and processes became digital.

But this is not a book about history, either of the North or photography. The journey of these photographs is through the modernity of life as it is lived along the Arctic Circle. Much is startling to those who live in the south, since for us it as an extreme world that we see here. But much is familiar. Everywhere people live with what the modern world has to offer, even if at times, and for profound reasons, they prefer or need to step into territories, of landscape, culture or the human imagination, that is outside and beyond modernity. As we look at these northern people looking out at us, we see both a welcome and fascination. This is the power and authority of these images, the remarkable achievement of a remarkable photographer.

Evgeny, Yamal

Thomas, Jetvik

Ivar, Træna

Madeline and Devin, Kotzebue

PORTFOLIO

NOTICE
AIRPORT PROPERTY ---- NO TRESPASSING
VIOLATORS WILL BE PROSECUTED

NO GUNS
OR
HUNTING
ON
AIRPORT PROPERTY

FORT YUKON
INSIDE THE ARCTIC CIRCLE
LAT. 66.34   LONG. 141.51
POP. SUMMER 800± WINTER 700±

ALASKA

Benjamin, Enoch and William, Fort Yukon

George, Kotzebue

Fannie, Eva and Velma, Fort Yukon

Jared, Kotzebue

◀ **Darce,** Kotzebue

Chasity, Fort Yukon

Summertime, Fort Yukon

◀ **John, Saima, Clara and Minni,** Kotzebue

Linda and Zool, Kotzebue

Stacey, Kotzebue

Ross, Kotzebue

Iva, Kotzebue

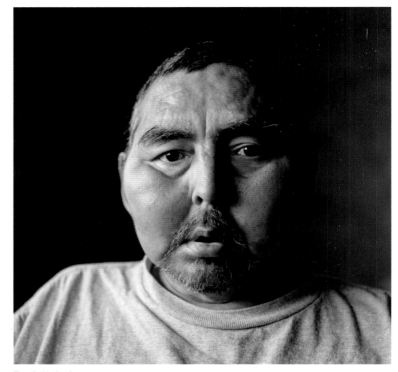

Paul, Kotzebue

William, Kotzebue

Josephine, Kotzebue

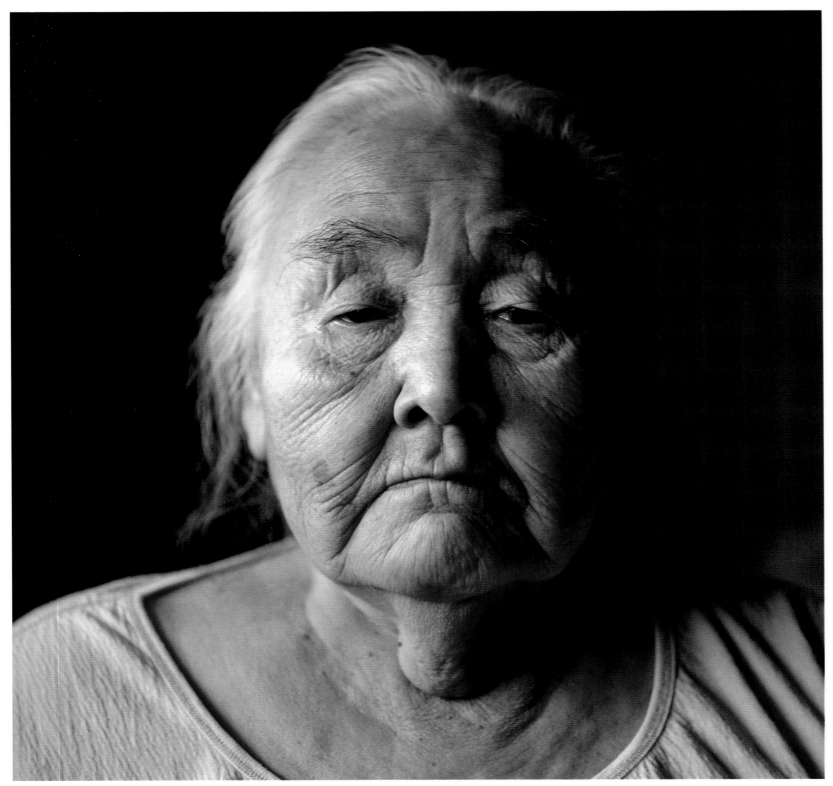

Nellie, Kotzebue

Hiram and Carrie, Kotzebue

Albert and family, Fort Yukon ▶

◄ **Brett,** Kotzebue

Clarence, Fort Yukon

Tabor, Thomas, McConnell and Nelson, Kotzebue

CANADA

◄ **Malvin,** Repulse Bay

Jamal, Repulse Bay

Modern Living, Repulse Bay

Paniak, Repulse Bay

Mary, Repulse Bay

Annie and daughter, Repulse Bay ▶

Daniel, Repulse Bay

◀ **Captain,** Davis Strait

Cecilia, Repulse Bay

◀ **Mark and George,** Sunshine Fjord

Mark, Pangnirtung

Bill, Sunshine Fjord

Boris, Pangnirtung

Madeleine, Pangnirtung

Crossing the Circle, Sunshine Fjord

Jacqueline and family, Repulse Bay

Bert and Sheri, Davis Strait ▶

►4   ►5   ►6

►7   ►8   ►9

GREENLAND

◄ **Graffiti,** Sisimiut

Kristian, Sisimiut

◂ **Maligiaq,** Sisimiut

Michael, Sisimiut

Christine, Sisimiut

Dorothy, Sisimiut

Dorthe and Ellen, Sisimiut

Loth, Sisimiut

Pavia, Sisimiut

Lars, Sisimiut

Inukkuluk and Nukannguaq, Sisimiut

ICELAND

◀ **Bjarni and Bjarni,** Grímsey

Garðar, Grímsey

Þöra, Raufarhöfn

Dagbjartur, Grímsey

Arni, Raufarhöfn

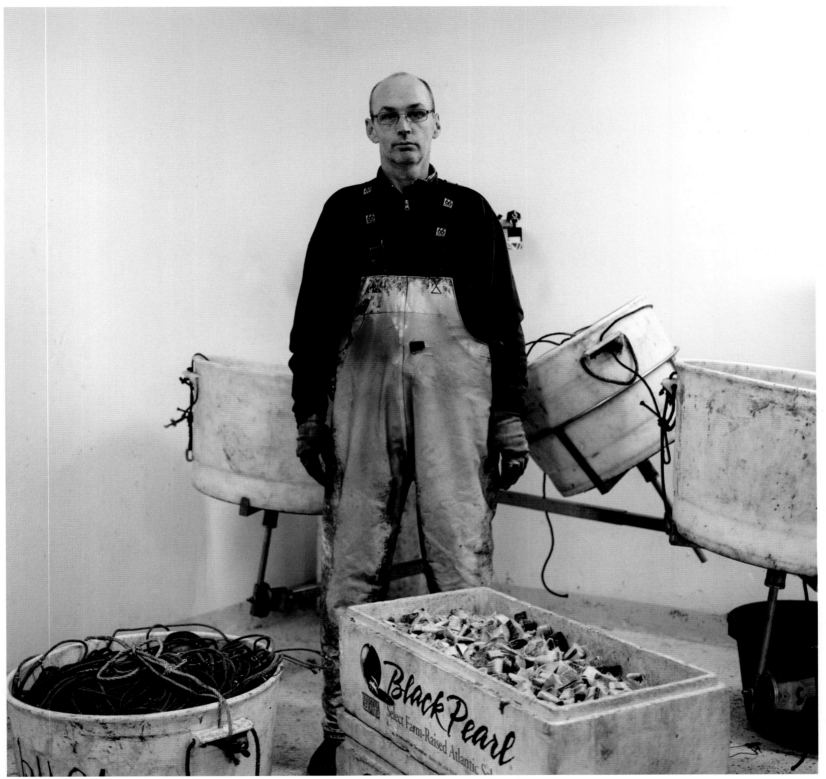

◄ **Kristin,** Raufarhöfn

Erlingur, Raufarhöfn

Alfreð, Grímsey

Ivar, Raufarhöfn ▶

NORWAY

Chapel, Rødøy

Roger, Træna ▶

◀ **Hans,** Rødøy

Home, Rødøy

Kirsti, Rødøy

Museum, Rødøy

Albert, Øresvik

Potatoes, Mo i Rana ▶

SWEDEN

◄ **Home,** Polcirkeln

Uwe, Murjek

Christopher, Jokkmokk

Nikolaus, Jokkmokk

Lars, Jokkmokk

Stefan, Jokkmokk

Tord, Jokkmokk

Thomas, Jokkmokk

◄ **Kurt,** Jokkmokk

◄ **Karl-Erik,** Jokkmokk

◀ **Annikka,** Övertorneå

Jan, Jokkmokk

FINLAND

◀ **Jaakko,** Rovaniemi

Katri, Posio

Erkki, Rovaniemi

Matti, Sonka

◂ **Pekka,** Ylitornio

Veikko, Rovaniemi

Risto, Rovaniemi

Jaakko, Rovaniemi

Home, Rovaniemi

Anu, Posio

Eini, Rovaniemi ▶

RUSSIA

Kostya, Yamal

Myangche, Yamal

Olga, Yamal

Nadyezhda, Yamal ▶

Firefighting, Old Umba

Victor and Rima, Old Umba

Auto Club, Tonya Tetrina

◀ **Lyudmilla,** Zhigansk

Kristina, Zhigansk

Lunch, Yar-Sale

Nargez, Yar-Sale

Zilya, Salekhard

Artyom, Zhigansk

Nikita, Kutopyugan

Stepan, Zhigansk

Prokopy and Nikolay, Zhigansk

Varga, Zhigansk

Ivan and Yevdokia, Zhigansk

Olga, Tonya Tetrina

Maria, Zhigansk ▶

Ganya, Zhigansk

Fyodrova, Zhigansk

Lyudmila, Zhigansk

Sergey, Labytnangi

Danil, Vika, and Lisa, Salekhard

Zlata and Tanya, Kuzreka

Northern Lights, Zhigansk

Maria, Zhigansk

◄ **Zinaida,** Zhigansk

Lyuda, Salekhard

Yuri, Zhigansk

Sergey, Zhigansk

NORTHERN JOURNEYS

Cristian Barnett and Huw Lewis-Jones

Cristian Barnett: I was born in Newcastle upon Tyne on April Fools' Day in 1971. Growing up I never imagined that I would travel far, let alone end up working right across the Arctic. I went to a failing comprehensive school and expectations weren't that high; to be a *photographer*, well, that just wasn't in our vocabulary. I studied part of my A-levels at the local college, which is how I came across the art faculty. Until that point I had never considered photography seriously as a career option. But I do remember the pleasure of studying with like-minded people for the first time in my life.

Huw Lewis-Jones: That's a step toward happiness isn't it — finding something that you enjoy and then discovering other people who share your creative interest. But, let's go back to the beginning; when do you think you first noticed photography?

CB: I was given a camera when I was about ten years old, a Kodak Ektra with flip-out handle and the blocks of bulbs. I even recall the smell of the box that the camera came in; I loved it. The anticipation of waiting for the prints to arrive by post was unbearable. My first adventure into taking photographs had very little to do with people or portraits though. Instead of taking the kind of photos that my family expected, I photographed things like tins of dog food from the kitchen cupboards. I had these little Star Wars toys and I built little film sets and photographed them. They were always out of focus because you could never get very close to a subject with the old instamatic. I think everyone was a bit surprised when they were developed to see quirky pictures of food tins and toys instead of family snapshots.

The first portrait I remember arranging was of my Nanna when I was about sixteen. She had a beautiful old Singer sewing machine and I shot her working on it and then printed it with a vignette to look like an old photograph. The kind of things people do so easily now with digital apps on their mobile phones. For me creating and printing a photograph remains a magical thing and it was important for me to learn this way, before digital photography overtook everything.

HLJ: Can you recall a photograph that changed your life, perhaps made you want to be a photographer?

CB: I know for sure that the first time I was profoundly moved by a photograph was when I visited Auschwitz in 1991. In one of the reconstructed huts was a display of hundreds of images that the Nazis took of the children as they were processed on arrival. The industrial scale of the display and repetition of photographs was only alarming once you began to carefully examine each picture, one at a time. There was a picture of a particularly beautiful young girl with an expressionless face. I wondered what the photographer thought as he took that picture, did he see her beauty and innocence, was he thinking about her inevitable fate, perhaps even his own children or family? In that one picture I could see the absolute worst of mankind. I still think they are the most shocking images I have ever seen.

HLJ: Looking back do you think that significant moment was the spark that made you want to become a photographer?

CB: I've never really thought too hard about a decisive moment like that, but I suppose it really was that important. I felt uncomfortable about the photographer's role in this — was he complicit, somehow to blame? I realized that photographs had a real power. They could be simple, or shocking, or so many things in between. That fascinated me, it still does. I began to experiment with portraiture and took many pictures that anyone familiar with my work would recognize as my style: simplicity, symmetry in composition, and within a setting that tells something of that person's life.

After a fairly demoralizing time as an advertising assistant (actually it was that bad, I thought many times about giving up), I then began working with two editorial photographers, one specializing in food and the other interiors. This two-year period had, without doubt, the biggest influence on my career. Released from the restraints of advertising I rediscovered my enthusiasm for photography and learned a new language of editorial storytelling. From then on, for most of my working life, I've been privileged to work in a creative industry with talented and enthusiastic people. It's impossible not to get excited about someone else's passion when they themselves are enthusiastic – whether it be growing sprouts, collecting spoons, or sailing round the world. Enthusiasm is a word I use time and again. If I lost it or had to work with people who don't have it then my career would be over.

HLJ: I think most people would agree with that. For me it's collaborating – be it curating exhibitions, creating books, or going out on expeditions into the wilderness – with people who are naturally curious about the world. The kind of people who answer a question and find there's much more to learn; people who want to see what's over the next range of hills, even after a long journey. That's a strong human impulse I think, and a good creative one too. We all enjoy traveling, but I know you prefer to spend days *not* photographing.

CB: Yes, I really don't want to take photographs just for the sake of a photograph. I do feel that we all tend to miss out on so many things when we travel simply because we become too focused on taking pictures. It narrows our frame. But that's also a little idealized as a viewpoint. When I'm working on a commission, or a very tight deadline for a shoot, of course photography becomes the driving force again. When on trips, I've seen so many times how a camera can have a negative effect on someone's experience of an environment, or an encounter. Not taking a photograph is so often the best

way to personally engage with something. I'd agree that's an odd thing for a photographer to say, but I stick by it.

When I travel I'm attracted far more to the people of an area than the landscape. It's a very special experience to be able to go somewhere for a few days and to spend that time going into people's houses. There are very few other scenarios in which that would be allowed to happen, or where people would welcome you in the same way. Photography can open doors, as much as you can imagine it might close them.

HLJ: Let's think a little more about the Arctic and what drew you there. The Arctic Circle threads its way over vast distances, an invisible line that runs through eight countries and a variety of landscapes. Tell us how the *Life on the Line* project came about?

CB: I was looking at the Arctic Circle on a map in an inflight magazine, simple as that. The idea came to me instantly and, almost as quickly, I realized I would need to devote a huge amount of time and money to try and bring it about. That was daunting to say the least, but I became intrigued – you might say a little obsessed – by the mysterious dotted line that dissected apparently vast empty spaces. It's a mathematical line of latitude 66 degrees and 33 minutes north of the Equator, intersecting various nations and, as you know, home to a rich diversity of people. There's magic in that for me. I was transfixed by the idea of the North and it cast a spell before I'd even got there. And that feeling of wonder has increased as I've come to understand it more.

HLJ: Tell me a little about your first journey?

CB: Well, the very first trip was to Finland in 2006. The idea was a simple one: photograph people on the Arctic Circle. I really had no greater ambition than that. I'd shoot everything on colour film with my medium-format Hasselblad. Working with a Finnish assistant we arranged some shoots in advance and met other people while there. This was the formula that I ended up using for the rest of the trips. The whole adventure seemed like my idea

Cristian, Sunshine Fjord

Reeta and Iikka, Rovaniemi

Pia, Sisimiut

Nikolai, Salekhard

of a perfect job – I was hooked. I loved turning up to meet people, spending some time talking with them, taking their picture and then making our way to the next location. It was a series of condensed experiences.

I found myself, in a way, being passed around a community and given opportunities to meet those people a community wanted me to meet. That certainly encouraged me to continue. There was also the haphazard, spontaneous element: the pure chance. The first photograph I made was of Timo, who was drilling a hole in the ice with what looked to me like a giant corkscrew. He was measuring the thickness of the frozen lake to check that it was still safe for cars to travel across. Even this seemed to me an extraordinary thing back then, to drive a car across a lake. I now know that travel across frozen ice, whether sea ice, lakes or rivers is a totally normal, indeed essential, thing in the Arctic during winter. Seven years later, I decided to make a final trip to Finland, the last for the whole project, and returned to meet Timo in his cabin. He was just finishing building it as winter was descending.

HLJ: We've used the phrase 'connecting and celebrating' to describe your impulse to photograph the people who live here. This ambition evolved over time, didn't it?

CB: *Life on the Line* is unashamedly positive. My aim is to celebrate the warmth and happiness that I've encountered here. If you want grim pictures of northern Russia, depressing images of unemployed Greenlandic youth it's easy enough to find them elsewhere. And you don't have to travel to the Arctic to create images that chime with the disenchantment of modern life. But what I found most interesting was to try and challenge stereotypes – my own included – to create a portrait of the Arctic that was honest and as I found it. I hope that this project will serve as a record of a snapshot of life at 66° 33′ 39″ N at this time in its history.

My second journey for this project was to Norway. From that point onwards I became very aware of the people I'd already met, living at this same latitude, and wondering what the connections were for these people. The idea of light, the extreme intensity of summer and winter, the remoteness and feeling of disconnection to the rest of the world perhaps, but also the closeness of a connection to the land and the environment. I admire the practicality of people and the appreciation of simple things. Obviously surface things like clothing, lifestyles, homes and food might show connections. It was nice to search for similarities as much as the range of difference.

I spend quite a lot of my working life photographing food so I also made a conscious decision not to involve any food in this project and I'm certainly no landscape photographer either. The reason I choose portraiture was for the experience of engaging with people. For me, travelling without meeting local people is not worth the trouble. I would rather have tea with a priest in Canada or share a bottle of Vodka on a train in Russia than visit any number of museums and galleries. My portraits are a by-product of these relationships; this is why I find quick-turnaround portraits generally unsatisfying.

HLJ: Certainly, if you invest the time in a genuine way the results are more interesting. Yet one of the key ingredients in this work is its spontaneity. That's something true of life in these communities but also the Arctic more generally – the unpredictability of things. But what can you say about the things that you found in common throughout the places you've visited?

CB: There are indigenous groups which span borders and obvious lifestyle similarities which come from living in what can be a difficult climate, but in my experience there are a couple of common threads running across the whole of the Arctic Circle. To varying degrees there is an alarming erosion of indigenous culture. In Canada I met a hunter in his late forties who was born in an igloo out on the tundra and lived a largely subsistence lifestyle in his childhood. The younger generation in his town would have all been brought up in houses and often have little or no interest in hunting. This cultural history is also the source of a frequently uneasy relationship between indigenous people and European incomers, which can manifest itself in outspoken hostility or quiet resentment. Sometimes this can also result in a crisis of identity.

On a more positive note though, I have found a warmth and hospitality throughout the whole of the Arctic that has really brought this project alive for me. I have been honoured to spend time among many Arctic people – the Gwichin, Saami, Khanti, Nenets, Evenks, Yakuts and Inuit – clearly

Nala, Kotzebue

Laurent, Repulse Bay

Rosalina and Tara, Repulse Bay

the Arctic Circle is much more than snow and polar bears. There are many thriving modern settlements where you are more likely to meet a hairdresser than a reindeer herder and there is much more diversity and happiness to life here than you might imagine.

HLJ: What advice could you offer someone wanting to shoot in the Arctic? Obviously extreme weather conditions are a given, but how best to thrive where other people might not?

CB: At the most basic level, the best advice is to keep yourself happy. Now that might mean taking lots of mosquito protection for the long summer, as much as you might expect me to say 'keep yourself warm'. This sounds obvious, but if you get cold you won't want to take pictures. Loading film and working with the camera is difficult with gloves and I often struggle to keep my hands from becoming too cold. To be honest though there were not too many days when I was seriously challenged by the weather. I only made 3 of the 13 trips in midwinter when conditions were difficult, other 'winter' trips were made in October or early April when the temperatures were easier to work in.

Knowing how your camera will react at different temperatures is also useful. My Hasselblad lenses work reasonably well down to about −15°C when the longer exposures become impossible. On my first *Life on the Line* trip, shooting in −20°C, I had two Blad lenses and one Mamiya lens stop working altogether. Earlier this year in Iceland, my 80mm was unable to work at anything slower than 1/4s. Fogging is also a problem when going indoors, so you must try to warm the camera slowly.

Setting myself that really narrow aim of shooting no further than 35 miles from the Arctic Circle obviously presented all sorts of problems, but for me that was a really good way to focus my efforts. This has meant I've been to many places that few people would have reason to visit. In Zhigansk, Russia, I was told that my translator and I were the 5th and 6th foreign visitors in almost a decade. Zhigansk is not a pretty place on the face of it and on arrival I was wondering how we would last the week. However, we made so many friends and had such a rewarding time that I was immensely grateful for the opportunity to visit.

HLJ: You've gone to great lengths to reach some remote places. Yet in many countries the Arctic Circle itself has become a draw hasn't it, a destination that has encouraged development simply because the interest of outsiders?

CB: That's right, it's peculiar, but I suppose I'm exactly one of those people to be drawn there. I think of Rovaniemi in Finland, a place pretty much defined by its location and the touristic pull is strong. You can explore 'Santa's Village' and post letters home stamped on the line. In some countries you find monuments or plaques. In many other places nothing at all. More recently hotel managers have been erecting signs and trying to drum up interest. In Grímsey, a little island off Iceland, you can jump over a piece of pipe that has been built to represent the line, so yes sometimes it's all a little meaningless, but it's always intriguing and often fun.

Travelling with the nomadic Nenets is something I'll treasure. We slept together in reindeer-skin tents. Yet it's not a lifestyle stuck in time. On my first night there most of the kids were watching films on small DVD players. It was not what I expected, but it was more interesting for me because it was real. Once I went fishing off the west coast in Greenland with an Inuit hunter. We went back to his apartment that night and he uploaded images he'd taken on his digital camera that day straight onto Facebook. His wife is the local hairdresser. In a way, they are more connected to the real world than I am.

HLJ: It's the young people with feet in both cultures, equally at home with gun, drum, or mobile phone in hand. In some places the old ways have been stamped out, or are in decline. In other places, there's a vibrancy to the new ways of doing things despite the many problems facing people. You remember that elder in Kotzebue who described going from 'stone age' to 'space age' in a generation? His mother had been born out on the tundra behind a rock and she had lived to watch men walk on the moon. These sorts of rapid cultural shifts are incredible to my mind.

CB: Stereotypes are easily found, but there is much to life here, and depth, without having to look too far. I'm drawn to the eccentric. In Kotzebue I photographed a man in a Jacuzzi, a woman growing vegetables. And why

Photo Shoot, Kotzebue

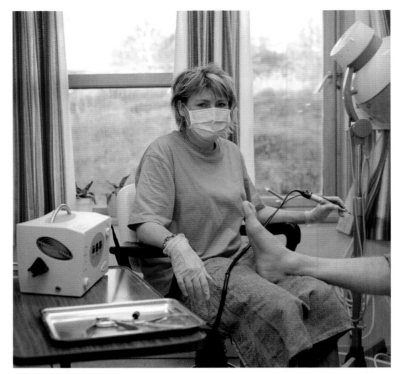

Eli, Træna

Yulia, Kola Peninsula

Arrival, Rovaniemi

not? Musical instruments, rooms full of books; these are all things that make winter life here more bearable, but for me they were like opening a door into people's lives. Hunters, artists, wrestlers, beauty-queens and elders.

Another thing I like to do is to give the person I'm photographing a Polaroid of their portrait, created on the spot. Many people think it a kind gesture. The encounter becomes a two-way process and something material too. Some are thrilled to have it. Some people don't even hold photographs anymore. I like to think that some of these little images might survive in the future, tucked into a shoebox or pinned to a wall. But, it's funny, sometimes people say thanks, but could I email it to them instead! They are more modern than I am, with my old-fashioned film and bulky apparatus.

HLJ: Ok, so when you are shooting in the Arctic what kit is most important?

CB: Well, speaking as a baldie - it's certainly a warm hat! Camera-wise, my typical Arctic kit is as follows: 1 Hasselblad, 2 lenses (80mm, 60mm), 2 backs (1 x 160ASA, 1 x 400ASA), Polaroid back, light meter, and a Mamiya 6. 80mm 2.8 is my preferred focal length. Other than that it's really nice to try and travel light. My three top tips, I suppose, would be: stay warm, make sure you have lots of credit available on a visa card and be prepared for big changes in your itinerary – don't plan to arrive home the day before that big shoot, you may not make it. The biggest problem I have now is that I lack the luxury of time, so I often feel pressure to capture a place and people with more haste than I would like. A large part of being on location is trying to decide how to represent a place in a small number of images and this is something I do worry about.

I remember first seeing an exhibition in Denmark in about 2002. I was struck by the contrast of early portraits of proud hunters and contemporary pictures of drunken youths playing pool. My first, naive impression was that Greenland was a country in the midst of depression with high unemployment and many social problems. Life in Greenland is far from perfect but my experience is in complete contrast to my first thoughts after seeing that exhibition. I have come to realize that it is often easier to take negative pictures rather than positive ones and this seems to be a route taken by many photographers working in the North, especially Russia.

I'm trying to create honest portraits of people within the places that are familiar to them – whether it's at home, work, amongst family, or out on the land. This is simple environmental portraiture. I think that's the best way I can describe it. I've never worked with a big 'artistic statement' in my head, or some sort of intellectual philosophy. As you know, I just enjoy meeting people. Some might say it's too simple but I know it works for me and, on the whole, the people that I meet and create images with seem to enjoy the process as much as I do. On rare occasions you can see beyond an image and into the soul of someone. That's something that I'm constantly searching for.

HLJ: To share these moments with people is a privilege for you as a photographer. And it has been an honour for me too, as your editor and companion in the field on these journeys. It doesn't matter sometimes if the image doesn't come out the way we want it, if the person you've photographed has had a positive experience.

CB: Exactly. A day spent when you didn't learn something is a day wasted. Photographing interesting people who impart something of themselves is always the most enjoyable thing to do with a camera. Collaboration and participation is a really important part of it. Without a willingness to be photographed, then you have nothing. The first questions I always ask are 'how would you like to be photographed?' or 'where would you like to be photographed?' What I hope people see from the portraits in our book is that many are quite proud and happy. People have been keen to show the world something of themselves. I also think, taken as a whole, these portraits become a strong statement about the Arctic in this place and time. I'm proud to have been part of that.

HLJ: This is a positive vision captured with respect, humour and light. When I look at these simple portraits, in these unknown faces, I feel an urgent call to attention. I see strong people, standing at the crossroads of tradition and modernity. Some communities have gone from the civilisation of the seal to the digital age in a single generation. They must now be in charge of their futures. Unlike other polar books, this is a statement of local people not a tale of Western explorers. Drawn to a vision of the empty Arctic, to adventure or struggle, some still forget the peoples who have thrived here for millennia. As outsiders, we should not only respect the wishes of local people, but also help them share and project their sense of the world.

Environmental problems will loom large in this 'progress at all costs' trajectory. Arctic waters are threatened with large-scale pollution. Protected zones in Alaska, Canada and Siberia are soon bound to be exploited, in spite of protests by ecologists. The oil companies and mining concerns, with their thousands of workers, are already poised to move in as the sea ice retreats and the permafrost melts. The scramble for resources is one reality that is gradually hitting the headlines, but the Western press rarely reports on the real human Arctic. The *life* of the people is overlooked.

The human and cultural costs of rapid change here really needs to be understood. It has been said that modernity in the Arctic is a crime of progress, a crime in process. But it would also be wrong to think that progress has brought the Inuit nothing but grief.

CB: I agree. I deliberately tried to meet people on their own terms. To travel in the Arctic does not have to be a grim struggle. And progress in the Arctic, with new development and new incomers, does not always mean problems and strife. But there is of course much care that is needed in the path that development takes.

HLJ: Inuit in every region of the Arctic have contrived at various times to adapt remarkably well. It is worth remembering that they moved skilfully from the harpoon, to the bow and arrow, to the rifle, from stone to steel, from dogs sleds to snowmobiles, from snow igloos to spacious wooden houses; they have also become experts in new technologies, using the Internet, embracing the digital age, connecting to others around the world like no previous time in their history.

Young Inuit aspire to extraordinary and radical change. The sacred drums meet rock music. American hip-hop, rap, break-dance and basketball are all now part of their blended culture. In the past the empowerment of the Inuit was agonizingly slow. An educated new generation understand quite

well that change came about too fast, too hastily, and without their voices being heard. Their parents were betrayed by progress. But they now have the ability to stand up and be heard. Whilst their elders remain conservative and cautious, the young are deeply involved in their own revolution.

Some people talk of the Arctic Circle as a gateway, and that is what it means to me. It's an imaginary place yet one that is, of course, very real; a place where the modern world and the natural world now meet and a place that faces an uncertain future. This is the Arctic as an inhabited place, or at least, small gatherings of humanity in a seemingly endless landscape. What is it about the Arctic environment, do you think, that is so special?

CB: I love the space of the Arctic. Sometimes you can be in a busy town but open tundra is within walking distance. The nearest town might be days away and some locations can be isolated for months during the year. I feel a freedom in these places. Perhaps it's a little like being at sea in the middle of the ocean: the promise of far horizons. But my experience of the Arctic has been brief and manageable, so I never see it as a scary, hostile space.

In winter, or at least on the edges of winter, the light is ethereal with a peculiar texture, other-worldly perhaps. In some cases the featureless land-scapes are just so massive that it's no surprise that I find the human elements interesting. Driving along the north coast of Iceland, coming to the end of this project, I experienced two of my favourite days. But there is no record; I met no people. It was midwinter and the conditions were severe, but mostly I was snug in the car as the storm raged outside. Had I done a trip like this at the start, I'm sure I wouldn't have felt so comfortable.

I sometimes feel that my photographs don't come close to illustrating the experience of the journey. However, a portrait can often tell a story in a way that writing can't. As humans we have an endless fascination with other people and the opportunity to look at another's face will always be interesting. The really *great* photographs (and I should say, I don't feel I've created one yet), capture such a special moment that it seems like something extraordinary is left hanging in the air. Ultimately, what excites me most about photography is that it allows me to go to places and do some things I would never be able to do without a camera – simple as that.

Trusteth in the Lord,
Kotzebue

AN ARCTIC YEAR

Ginny Alexander

Many people outside think of the Arctic as a dark place. In actual fact, one of the main delights of living north here in Alaska is the wonderful variety in the light. In spring we don't just gain a few seconds a day: we gain minutes. Before we know it, we've gained hours and hours. Darkness becomes a memory. The sun is with us. There are marvellous sunrises and sunsets that linger so long that you can't tell when the sunset ends and the sunrise begins. It is as though the sun is reluctant to leave.

Fort Yukoners are solar-powered. The good old sun is shining down on us for more hours every day now, and each day we feel more of its warmth. It seeps into our bones and warms us all the way through. It wakes us in the morning and nudges us out of bed – happily. No more moaning and groaning and crawling deeper under the quilt. We look at the thermometer – not to see how cold it is, but rather how warm. We have stopped wearing three pairs of mittens and have traded up canvas boots for tennis shoes. Is this the day we can stop wearing long-johns? Any reason or no reason is a good excuse to be outdoors. The weather is perfect for driving dogs or snow-machining; ice skating or target shooting; walking and visiting; skiing and sledging and cutting wood and maybe even hanging out the laundry. People seem thinner. They are no longer wearing huge amounts of clothing. Does the sun make them happier, or is it that now we can see the smiles that have been hidden under scarves all winter? Wherever you go in Fort Yukon you'll see people outdoors soaking up the sun, recharging their batteries.

April is my kind of month. It's the kick back, relax and watch-the-snow-melt month. It's too late for winter and too early for summer. The weather is perfect. Gone is the biting cold. April has snowbirds and no mosquitoes. What could be more perfect? April is the month that gives us a sense of wellbeing. We silently pat ourselves on the back for having survived another

Ginny, Fort Yukon

winter and we tell ourselves that it wasn't that tough. We look forward to what nature has to offer in the coming spring and fall and know that all is well in our little corner of the world. Maybe April should be sixty days long?

★ ★ ★

'Doctor, lawyer, merchant, chief…?' One of the attractions of a village such as Fort Yukon is that you can be anything you want to be. Most of us don't exactly plan on being a 'doctor' or an 'accountant', or whatever. Joe Blow fixes his snowmachine. Then he fixes someone's ATV. Pretty soon he IS a mechanic. No certificate. Maybe not even any training. Just experience. Joe probably never intended to be a 'mechanic', but he tried it, liked it, and does it. A lot of us fall into jobs this way. Something needs doing. Someone does it. Eventually each of us finds the job that suits us and that we are suited for. Some of us are even fortunate enough to get the training we need to do the job properly, in which case we don't have to re-invent the wheel. Health aides across Alaska have been instrumental in saving lives and relieving suffering. They are not 'doctors', but they definitely fill the role in bush communities.

You have good penmanship? You're the unofficial sign maker and cake decorator. You know some chords on the guitar? Play and we'll dance. You read the Bible? Lead our Sunday service. You understand forms? Help me fill out my income tax return. We don't have a certificate on the wall that says we are a baker or a preacher or an accountant; but we bake and preach and do the accounting. One woman here is a school teacher, Lay Reader, the Avon representative, the weather woman, an EMT, the customs official and is getting her pilot's licence. She is also a terrific gardener. Solder, sailor, tinker, tailor. It's up to you.

Nick, Davis Strait   **Anton,** Yar-Sale   **Arnold,** Zhigansk

Contrary to popular opinion, fishing is not the No. 1 summertime activity here in Fort Yukon. This honour goes to bug-battling. While there are a great number of people who do fish in the summer, there is an even greater number who battle bugs. In particular, they battle mosquitoes. The most common weapon against bugs is 'Alaska Cologne' – mosquito dope that we spray or rub on ourselves to keep the wee beasties at bay. Then there is the traditional method, which consists of pulling a small branch off a willow and swishing it around yourself. This works, but unfortunately while you are swishing around your left leg the mosquitoes are biting your right ear; and while you swish near your right ear, the mosquitoes are emptying all the blood out of your left elbow. There is no escape from these tiny monsters. Despite screens on your door and windows, the mosquitoes pack their bags and move into your house where they continue to bug you. The one thing that really keeps the bugs away is our 70 below zero cold. No wonder Alaskans are so fond of winter.

Construction season is now upon us. Chicken wire is in great demand. Nails are selling by the bagful. Plywood, lumber, poles and logs can be seen on the back of trucks. All throughout Fort Yukon you can see people building fishwheels – those wonderful, graceful, efficient, simple machines that are used to harvest the abundant salmon that will soon swim up the Yukon. It is a real delight to watch these machines being constructed. Soon these marvellous water powered machines will be making their soft groaning sounds as they slowly turn and scoop up the salmon.

Some people are working on their new homes. Most of these are made from logs. Some people are able to finish their house in a year, but generally it takes more time than that. The first summer is usually spent getting and peeling the logs and laying the foundation. The second summer is spent putting up the walls and roof. The third summer is spent doing all the inside work. By the time the fourth year comes, your needs have changed and you have to add on – a new entry here, more electrical outlets there, and so on. Some people are getting running water installed. As any homeowner knows, a house is never finished.

Boat construction and repair is also in full swing. Riverboats are as essential to a Fort Yukoner as a car is to someone who lives in the city. They are used for work and pleasure. The river is home to many people here. Finally, there are all those little odds and ends that crop up during the summer – a fence around the garden, a basketball court over here, a drying rack there. Saws zing out their songs. Hammers tap-dance on nail heads. The terrific aroma of fresh cut lumber and the poignant smell of paint and varnish fill the air.

★ ★ ★

'The king salmon are coming', says the wind. It starts off gentle enough and then it increases in strength and velocity. It blows harder and harder and then it abates. The king salmon are coming. The fluff from the cottonwood trees flies, not just a little bit, but like a snowstorm. Some older people say this is food for the fish, so the king salmon should be here soon. 'The king salmon are coming', says the river. The colour of the water changes. It's no longer a rippled reflection of the sky and shore. When the king salmon come, the river turns a milky colour. The old man smells the smoke from the wood splash. The kings are here.

It's time for Fish Camp. Our camps are as different as the individuals who inhabit them. About the only thing that all the fish camps have in common are smoke houses, a cutting table, several knives, a file, fish and, of course, lots of innovation. Some fish camps are quite simple. These usually have a tent, sleeping bags, extra clothing, dishes, a place to cook and some food. From this start most fish camps grow in complexity. Tent frames are built. Chairs and benches, some very ingenious, are made. Foam mattresses, cots and sometimes beds are brought in. Floors of the tent are covered with spruce boughs. If a tent frame has been put up, there might actually be a wooden floor.

Kitchens vary from camp to camp more than anything else. There is usually a table. Sometimes it's a folding card table. Frequently it is a table or shelf made on the spot. Storage arrangements include a grub box, shelves and a means of hanging things up in the air. The fireplace, too, goes from the extremely simple (a place where a few sticks of wood can be burned) to the more elaborate. Most camps have some kind of grill. A Dutch oven is considered a must by many camp cooks. All sorts of other ovens have been contrived. Biscuits, cakes, cobblers and many an elaborate concoction have

Jason, Kotzebue   **Greg and Patricia,** Kotzebue   **Miki,** Posio

been baked in these. Some people have set up spits where they slow roast their meat or fish as they sit around and chat.

Fall is a very satisfying season. The sights and sounds and smells of fall have all other seasons beat hands down. The berries are ripe out there and ready for the picking. About the only thing that can beat the smell of highbush cranberry jelly is the fresh bread that you spread the newly-made jelly on. The sight of sunlight streaming through the cooling jars of jelly is on a par with the finest stained glass windows of Europe.

The work of king salmon season is over, but the rewards are evident everywhere. Freezers are full of whole salmon, salmon steaks, salmon fillets. Caches are full of the rich pungent odour of smoked salmon and piles of dried salmon. Inside and outside people are cooking up more salmon. Then there are the vegetables. People have been enjoying the veggies from their gardens for several weeks now. Soon you will see small mountains of potatoes spread out to dry on people's floors, getting dry for winter storage. Of course, there are new potatoes boiling on the stove to go along with those salmon steaks and zucchini bread. In the coolest place in the house plants might be hanging from the rafters. As each tomato ripens it is plucked and eaten.

Although the wildflowers are pretty much gone for the year, people with flower gardens are enjoying petunias and pansies, straw flowers and clarkias, bachelor buttons and poppies. Even roses are in evidence. The leaves have started to change from a rather monotonous green to brilliant reds and yellows and oranges. Soon those bare spots in the yards will be filled with wood. Cords of wood will be stacked high – each person making a guess as to how long and how cold the coming winter will be and figuring how much wood they will need to fight off the cold until next spring.

Hunting season is almost upon us. People are looking forwards to filling another freezer with moose meat, ducks and geese. Most of them won't succeed because they are lucky. They will succeed because they are good hunters and aren't afraid of hard work and they only take what they think they will need. Luck plays a part, but skill has the starring role. Every year discussions turn to who has the most work to do – the men who hunt and kill the moose or the women who cut and pack away the moose. Many men cannot understand what there is to discuss. It's obvious to them that the

men have to do all the dirty work. After all they are the ones who have to prepare everything for the trip. They have to decide where the moose will be and what hunting strategy to use. They have to pack the boat and drive it and make sure that they don't break down.

It is the men who have to be able to shoot the huge beasts and who have to skin them; and cut them into portable parcels; and pack them back to the boats; and bring them back to town before they spoil. It is the men who have to walk through the mud and the rain with hundreds of pounds of meat on their backs. It is so obvious. The men have to do all the dirty work when it comes to moose hunting while the women sit at home in front of a warm fire.

Some women, too, feel that there is really nothing to discuss. It is obvious that the women have to do the dirty work when it comes to getting the moose. After all, they are the ones who spend days getting things ready for the men to take. They make sure that they have the groceries that will be needed; that the camping pots are together and clean; that the warm socks and the down parkas don't have any holes in them. All this while the men are sitting around chit-chatting and maybe picking up the gas. While the men are out having a ball on the river zipping around in the sunshine, it is they – the women – who are keeping things running smoothly at home.

They have to take care of the kids; keep the fire burning; cook the meals; clean the house; change the propane tank (propane tanks never run out when the men are in town); feed the dogs, and so many other things. Then when the men get back from their little 'vacation' on the river, it is the women who have to cut the hundreds of pounds of meat into steaks and soup bones and stew meat; package it; label it; and put it into the freezer (although it is true that some men are great about helping with this). Then the women have to clean and put away all the hunting gear. It is obvious to some of the women – they have to do all the dirty work while the men get to have all the fun. When it comes to moose hunting, what's to discuss?

★ ★ ★

It is always hard at this time of the year to believe that 600 people actually live in Fort Yukon. There is almost no activity on the street. The number of

Mike, Repulse Bay

Emil, Murjek

Pooyne, Yar-Sale

Sveta, Yamal

people attending church or going to the store drops rapidly. It must be fall time. Many people are out shopping on the Yukon. They are getting their moose and caribou, their ducks and geese. If they want to eat meat this winter, they must get it now.

Others are bringing back boat-loads of fish from their fish camps. They spent all summer drying it and now it's ready. The berries and rosehips are being gathered and turned into jelly and sauces. Some of the older people are gathering sage and plants for medicinal uses. The woodchoppers are busy getting as many cords of wood as they can before the cold weather sets in. It's very reassuring to look at your yard and see a huge pile of wood just sitting there ready for you to use when old man winter comes to visit. The fire fighters are out, too – way out. Many have gone to the Lower 48 to help fight the fires that are ravaging that part of the country.

The first big snowfall of the season is always cause for joy amongst the kids. When they first see those little white flakes fall they can hardly contain themselves. They run to one window, 'Yes, it looks like snow!' Then, invariably, they run to another window – just to make sure. And the mad rush is on – where are my hat, mittens and scarf, parka, snowsuit and heavy socks and boots? Never mind that the temperature is actually only a few degrees colder than it was an hour ago, they need every one of these items right now.

Most of the adults, too, are happy to see the snow. Not only is it a reaffirmation that all is well with Mother Nature, but it is like an old friend that has come to visit. The world is brighter. Sounds are muted. There is a beauty that all share. We know in the back of our minds that we are not really ready for winter. There is that window that should have been fixed. The saw-horse isn't ready yet; those things if left out in the yard won't to be seen again until next spring.

It's that roly-poly time of year. On go the long johns. On go the heavy pants, T-shirt, turtleneck sweater, flannel shirt – that should do the trick. On go the first pair of socks, then the second. Now, I'm ready to get dressed. On go the knit socks, then the caribou legging boots. Now the snow pants, the scarf, the parka and the marten hat. Finally a pair of gloves and the beaver mitts. Of course, no one can actually walk with all this on. It's time for the fifty degree below zero roly-poly waddle.

Christmas Approaches. The rich tones of church bells call us to celebrate the birth of Christ. And celebrate we do! The churches are packed. Extra chairs are placed down the centre of the aisle. The true spirit of Christmas is within us. After the church service we all exchange greetings and gifts.

The women have been sewing for months so that their children and grandchildren can have new canvas or caribou legging boots. Gorgeous beaded gloves and slippers are given to loved ones. Many people are wearing brightly knitted scarves and new handmade parkas. People of all ages are wearing warm marten hats. These beautiful gifts bring joy to the giver, the receiver and to all who see them. It is a pleasure to see these brightly coloured works of art worn with dignity by people walking along snow covered trails and surrounded by spruce trees. We don't really miss the busy sidewalks.

When you put on a pair of caribou legging boots, it's like putting on a pair of dancing feet. They are extremely lightweight. Wearing them is like a cross between being barefooted and walking on air. Besides keeping your feet warm when the temperature is 30 below zero or colder, they always look terrific. I can't decide if they look best on little kids who never seem to walk when they are wearing them. They bounce. They dance. They twirl and slide. Or maybe they look best on young adults. People wearing them seem to stand taller and straighter. They don't exactly look formal, but they do look elegant.

Or maybe caribou legging boots look best on our elders. They frequently indicate the background of the person wearing them. Some show the influence from Old Crow, Canada, or Arctic Village. The elders wearing caribou legging boots seemed to have a spring in their step that belies their age. What a great invention caribou legging boots are. They keep our toes snuggly warm in the coldest of weather. They delight the eye and the bright tassels and beadwork and add colour to the winter scene. They warm our feet and our heart. But, as the years have passed, I'm seeing less of the caribou boots and homemade parkas, or the beautiful fur hats, and ruffs and beaded gloves. Carhartt brown and black is the order of the day amongst the young.

One shaft of light, then another, and more and more, pierce the darkness as many one-eyed monsters spring to life. Something from the Twilight Zone? No, it's just people leaving a gathering – whether it's bingo, school, a meeting, or whatever. The one-eyed monsters are snowmobiles. What a boon they have been for the rural communities. We can slip down to the store or to the school. We can go on winter picnics or to trap lines. We can even go to other villages. In fact, we can go almost anywhere there is snow. These wonderful machines have certainly made life easier for the people in small villages. We use them to haul everything – the extra groceries we get from the store; the water we drink; the wood with which we heat our homes; everything. These iron dogs have replaced the flesh and blood kind as far as transportation here on the Arctic Circle goes.

★ ★ ★

Fort Yukoners used to love it when we received the 'Fickle Finger of Frigidity Award'. People who lived elsewhere would look at their TV and say to themselves: 'Thank God I don't live there!' (And we thought the same thing – 'Thank God they don't live here. We don't need their problems.') We used to be the cold spot quite often but it's been a long time since Fort Yukon had that honour. It does still get cold here. Life trucks along at pretty much a normal speed down to about 30 below zero or so. At 38 below most of the cars grow square wheels and snow machines refuse to start. At 55 below the planes no longer fly. No mail; no supplies; no visitors; no new diseases.

The kids may think it is too cold to go to school at 55 below, but that doesn't stop them from going to the post office or the AC store. At 70 below zero, which we haven't seen much of in the last few years, things definitely slow down – especially the oil. Heating oil tends to turn to jelly at that temperature. That's the main reason people used to have a wood stove that they could substitute for their oil stove. People also have more of a tendency to stay home at 70 below. To tell the truth, after a few days of 70 below, 30 below seems positively warm. Your eyelashes no longer freeze together. Your forehead doesn't feel like someone is throwing ice darts at it. Movement in the fingers and toes once again becomes more than just a memory. Is it global warming that is starting to make Fort Yukon look like the Banana Belt of the Arctic?

However, one of the worst things about the Arctic is when Mother Nature does something out of character – for example, rain in January. Totally unexpected. We are not ready for it. Until we slip, or until we go to get wood and find it frozen in a lump of ice, the reality hasn't sunk in. At 70 below we know what to do. Rain in January? A whole new ball game. The biggest challenge facing us now is climate change. It is steadily getting warmer, wetter, and windier here – all things that are new to us. We are having to learn to deal with this as are the animals and fish that we used to rely on. It seems to me that, on average, the temperature has risen one degree for each year I have been here. We haven't seen 80 below in over four decades. The 70s below are mere memories. This year only two days of 50 below. With all the new technology and the changes in the weather, we are going to have to figure out what jobs will be needed in the future and plan for this.

Some people go on believing that we sit huddled in the dark and cold for six months of every year. Keep it to yourself that it is sometimes possible to read a newspaper outdoors just from the light of the stars and the northern lights and the moon reflecting off the snow. You can mention that all this darkness causes depression in some people, but don't tell them about the thousands of people on the Arctic Circle who actually like the darkness, especially after all those months of nothing but sunshine. Beware, too, of the vegetarians. If they ever find out that there are places in the Arctic that have more hours of sunlight during the growing season than anywhere else on earth and that we can grow not only huge, but tasty, vegetables they may want to make a run for our borders.

Under the Arctic blue skies of Fort Yukon, I am happy. Life always changes, everything is always in flux. In some ways it is better, in other ways not so good. People no longer need fear starvation. Not only are all the old resources still available, there is a whole host of new things we can use. We have more choices today – heat from wood or oil? Beef or moose? Employment or self-reliance? Most of us choose a little of both. Our community is extreme, but we are free and nature here is still bountiful and diverse. We pray that it will remain so. The Arctic Circle is an imaginary line drawn by someone I don't know, a mathematical concept made for a map. Yet the people and the landscape of the Arctic Circle is what's real to me: freedom and change, opportunity and challenge. When you work with nature you're in for a great life.

Oline, Itilleq

INDEX

2   3   4   5   6   7   8   9   10   11   12   13

14   15   16   17   18   19   20   21   22   23   24   25   26   27

28   29   30   31   32   33   34   35   36   37   38   39   40   41

P52 Mary Qulitalik from Igloolik is visiting family in Repulse Bay. 2010.

P53 Annie Angotialuk carries her daughter in the hood of her traditional amauti, Repulse Bay. 2010.

P55 Daniel Szwarc is a priest at the Roman Catholic Mission in Repulse Bay. 2010. An Inuit sledge makes for a beautiful altar.

P56 From the bridge of his ship *Akademik Ioffe*, Captain Gennadiy Poskonniy scans the horizon for icebergs. Photographed at sea in the Davis Strait, crossing from Baffin Island to the west coast of Greenland. 2013.

P57 Cecilia Angotialuk enjoys a cigarette as we talk in her home, Repulse Bay. 2010.

P58 Mark Robinson and George Kourounis are storm-chasers on assignment from Canada's Weather Network. Shooting a piece to camera in Baffin Island's Sunshine Fjord, George decides to wear a horse's head – and why not? 2013.

P59 Mark Kilabuk is a volunteer fireman at Pangnirtung, Baffin Island. 2013.

P60 It's a long way from California for adventurous tourist Bill Collins, shot here in Baffin Island's Sunshine Fjord. It was a pleasure to have my photograph taken by Bill as he'd studied under the great Ansel Adams in the 1950s. 2013.

P61 Expedition leader Boris Wise rides the bosun's chair as his Zodiak is craned onto the waters of the fjord at Pangnirtung. 2013.

P62 Madeleine Qumuatuq, Pangnirtung. 2013.

P63 Guests on the ship *Akademik Ioffe* gather on the bow to celebrate crossing the Arctic Circle in Baffin Island's Sunshine Fjord. 2013.

P64 Jacqueline Putulik, Repulse Bay. 2010.

P65 Fresh from the Russian sauna onboard the *Akademik Ioffe*, Bert Ritchie and Sheri Almond are about to brave the freezing plunge pool. It's a nice way to mark crossing the Arctic Circle in the middle of Davis Strait!

GREENLAND

P68 Graffiti, Sisimiut. 2013.

P69 Master carver Kristian Skifte takes a pipe break, working in his studio down by the Sisimiut harbourside. 2013.

P70 Maligiaq Enoksen Olsen, Sisimiut. 2013.

P71 Michael Johansen and his kayak, Sisimiut. 2013.

P72 Museum director Christine Løventoft-Jessen stands on the steps of the Bethel Church, consecrated in 1775 and one of Greenland's oldest. Sisimiut. 2013.

P73 Polar bear enthusiast, American Dorothy Harpster at the Sisimiut museum. 2013.

P75 Sisters Dorthe Kruse and Ellen Kruse Henningsen have just been celebrating their niece's first day at school. Glass beads arrived in Greenland in the nineteenth century as trade items, and they have been used in decorative clothing ever since. 2013.

P76 Sisimiut artist Loth Sorensen is famed locally for his mask carvings. 2013.

P77 Pavia Ludvigsen and his Batman headphones, Sisimiut, Greenland. 2013.

P78 On the first day of the school year in Sisimiut, new entrants and their families arrive in traditional clothing. It's a proud day for Nuunukkuluk Berthelsen. 2013. Her kamik 'boots' are made of seal skin.

P79 The first person I met in Greenland, Sulli lives in Sisimiut. He is a passionate breakdancer. 2013

P80 Lars Lennert Soerensen is a lifeguard at the outdoor pool in Sisimiut during the very brief summer. 2013.

P81 Inukkuluk G. Lennert is the youngest Taekwando black belt in Greenland and the star of the family. Life is probably a little tough for his older brother Nukannguaq. Sisimiut, 2013.

ICELAND

P84 Bjarni Magnússon, lighthouse keeper and his grandson Bjarni, Grímsey. 2009.

P85 Garðar Alfreðsson hunting puffins, Grímsey. 2009.

P87 Þóra Soffía Gylfadöttir smiles through the window of her Raufarhöfn gallery. Not many visitors at this time of the year. 2013.

P88 Dagbjartur Einarsson, Grímsey. 2009.

P89 Farmer Arni Gunnarsson tends to his Icelandic sheep. Despite being a very hardy breed, they now spend the harsh Arctic winter indoors. They are bred both for their meat and wool, which makes a great jumper.

Arni says: 'I was born here in Iceland on a farm that my father and grandfather worked before me. I now look after over five hundred sheep. On the land you can be your own man, away from the noise and traffic of the city. To my mind there is nothing bad about living here. The winters are long, but the northern lights are mesmerising and when spring returns everything comes back to life. I'd like the world to know how beautiful it is here to be close to nature; we have peace and togetherness in this simple way of life.' Raufarhöfn. 2013.

P90 Kristin Palsdöttir, assistant in the only store in town open in winter. Raufarhöfn. 2013.

P91 Garðar Friðgeirsson is baiting the fishing lines, waiting for an improvement in the winter weather before the fleet heads to sea. Raufarhöfn. 2013.

P93 Hotelier Erlingur B Thoroddsen stands at the 'Arctic Henge', built on a hill overlooking Raufarhöfn. 2013.

P94 Alfreð Garðarsson looks after the Grímsey church. 2009.

P95 Putting up the Christmas lights in Raufarhöfn is a cold job, so handyman Ivar Sigthorsson is prepared for the worst. 2013.

98 99 100 101 102 103 104 105 106 107 108 109 110 111
112 113 114 115 116 117 118 119 120 121 122 123 124 125
126 127 128 129 130 131 132 133 134 135 136 137 138 139
140 141 142 143 144 145 146 147 148 149 150 151 152 153

NORWAY

P98 Petter Dass chapel, Træna. 2007.

P99 Roger Møen, farmer and owner of what might be the most northerly herd of Herefordshires in the world. Træna. 2007.

P100 Asbjørn Steinsrud, Fisherman, Øresvik. 2007.

P101 Reidun Arntsen, Rødøy. 2007.

P102 Hans Roger Pedersen, ambulance boat captain, Rødøy, 2007.

P103 Håkon Arntsen, Coastal Museum, Rødøy. 2007.

P105 At the water's edge, Rødøy. 2007.

P106 Kirsti Tengøy, owner of 'The Little Gallery', Rødøy. 2007.

P107 Inside the Coastal Museum, Rødøy. 2007.

P108 Albert Hilstad, 'Fjord Postman', Øresvik. 2007

P109 Potatoes for sale, near Mo i Rana. 2007.

SWEDEN

P112 A little home for birds, Polcirkeln. 2007.

P113 Uwe Schmidt, a German who retired to live in Murjek. 2007.

P114 Bo Larsson, Polcirkeln. 2007.

P115 Christopher Larsson, ice hockey player, Jokkmokk. 2007.

P117 Nikolaus Kitok, selling Sami arts at the winter festival, Jokkmokk. 2010.

P118 Lars Pirak, artist, yoiker and master carver, a man who had done so much for Sami culture, Jokkmokk. 2007. I was sad to learn of his death the following year.

P119 Stefan Rutström, taxidermist, winter market, Jokkmokk. 2010.

P120 Tord Enlund, classic car enthusiast, near Jokkmokk. 2010.

P121 Sami elder Thomas Marainen at the Jokkmokk winter market. 2010.

P122 Kurt Lennart Stenman with moose target, Jokkmokk. 2010.

P123 Karin, florist, Jokkmokk. 2007.

P124 Karl-Erik Vesterberg, trapper, Jokkmokk. 2010.

P125 Lars Anders Håkansson, tanner, Jokkmokk. 2007.

P126 Annikka Tuohino, taking a dip in a hot tub, Övertorneå. 2007.

P127 Jan Sjöblom attends the winter market dressed in his grandfather's wolf coat, Jokkmokk. 2010.

FINLAND

P130 Jaakko Ollila, stock-car racer, Rovaniemi. 2006.

P131 Maria Manninen, fashion student, Rovaniemi. 2013.

P132 Katri Konttinen, student, Posio. 2013.

P133 Erkki Orre, racing reindeer trainer, Rovaniemi. 2006.

P135 Matti Härkönen ice-church builder, Sonka. 2006.

P136 Pekka Lovikka is a renowned kantele maker, the Finnish national instrument, Ylitornio. 2006.

P137 Veikko Heiskari, reindeer farmer, near Rovaniemi. 2013

P138 Risto Maijanen, hotel manager, Rovaniemi. 2006.

P139 Jaakko Gauriloff, Sami singer, Rovaniemi. 2006.

P141 A cosy caravan in Rovaniemi. 2006.

P142 Anu Pentik, celebrated Finnish ceramic artist, Posio. 2013.

P143 Eini Marja, wine-maker, Rovaniemi. 2006.

RUSSIA

P146 Ilya Segeyev's Gaz van is getting a check over, Zhigansk. 2013.

P147 Student Anatoly Galushkin also likes 'tricking', a form of acrobatic martial arts. Zhigansk. 2013.

P148 Nenet herder Kostya is drinking the blood of a newly-killed reindeer, Yamal Peninsula. 2012.

P149 Myangche Serotetto sits on one of the many reindeer sledges that are used by the nomadic Nenets as they move across the Yamal Peninsula. 2012.

P150 Olga playing in a children's 'chum', the traditional Nenets tent, Yamal Peninsula. 2012.

P151 Nadyezhda gathers wood for the cooking stove, Yamal Peninsula. 2012.

P152 Firefighting equipment at a fish farm, Old Umba. 2011.

P153 Victor and Rima, Old Umba. 2011.

P155 Members of the St Petersburg 'Automachinistov Club' stop for a group portrait, on crossing the Arctic Circle at Tonya Tetrina. 2011.

P156 Alexeeva Lyudmilla Goergievna, sewing group, Zhigansk. 2013

P157 Pavlova Kristina Igorovna, sewing group, Zhigansk. 2013

P158 It's raw reindeer jaw for lunch, Yar-Sale. 2012.

P159 Nargez, waiter, Yar-Sale. 2012.

P160 Zilya, a local taxi driver, really wanted to have her photograph taken on this huge concrete mammoth, which welcomes visitors to the Siberian city of Salekhard. 2012.

P161 Artyom Fyodorov, Zhigansk. 2013.

P162 Nikita, hunter, Kutopyugan. 2012.

P163 Stepan Lvov cooks lunch in the forest outside of Zhigansk. 2013.

P165 Prokopy Petrov and Nikolay Egorov, both residents of the elders' home, stand proudly with their medals, Zhigansk. 2013.

P166 Farmer's son Varga Solomonova and his cow, Zhigansk. 2013.

P167 Ivan Kilyabitov and Yevdokia Shadrina at the elders' home, Zhigansk. 2013.

P168 On the shores of the White Sea at Tonya Tetrina there is a small museum encampment. Russian tourist Olga meets me, having washed her pots at the beach. 2011.

P169 Maria Ivanova, Zhigansk. 2013.

P170 Clockwise from top left: Ganya Vladimirov in wood-work class, Zhigansk. 2013; Fyodrova's hotel, the only one in Zhigansk, hosts these popular pool tables. 2013; Sergey Jurylo, electrician and amateur weightlifter, Labytnangi. 2012; Lyudmila Stepanova teaches at the Children's Art School in Zhigansk. 2013.

P171 In Salekhard, Danil, Vika, and Lisa are rehearsing for the school play. 2012.

P173 Zlata and Tanya, Kuzreka. 2011.

P174 The Northern Lights 'Severenoye Sviyanie' dance ensemble gather having just returned from a tour to Holland. Zhigansk. 2013.

P175 Maria Ivanova, Zhigansk. 2013.

P176 Zinaida Anatolyevna Orgutsova, at church in Zhigansk. 2013.

P177 Lyuda, a Khanty woman who works hard to promote her cultural heritage, Salekhard. 2012.

P178 Yuri Raspopov, engineer at the Zhigansk power station. 2013.

P179 Sergey Pavlov plays the drums for the local dance troupe, Zhigansk. 2013.

P180-81 A curious reindeer peers into shot at a Nenets camp, Yamal. 2012.

DISCUSSION & REFLECTION

P182 A bridge near Kópasker on the north coast of Iceland. 2013.

P185 Photographer Cristian Barnett setting up his camera, Sunshine Fjord. 2013.

P186 Left to right: Reeta Kerola and Iikka Kupari cool off in the winter night after a sauna in Rovaniemi. 2013; One of the first things to strike you as you arrive in Greenland are the vibrant colours of the wooden houses. At the technical college in Sisimiut, teacher Pia Olsen instructs the next generation of local decorators to continue this tradition. 2013; Nikolai, near Salekhard. 2012.

Iikka says: 'I moved to the Arctic Circle, to Rovaniemi, over a decade ago having fallen in love with a girl. I come from the Finnish countryside and I had to get used to the Arctic life quickly. That first winter we had -40°C for many weeks. Weather like that motivates you to learn fast how to dress when you go out. I'm now working as a systems analyst at the University of Lapland and think of the Arctic as my home. The community is positive and traditional, though we're not all hunters here in the Arctic. Nature is so close – we have wide, wild forests in all directions – but I've never hunted anything but mosquitoes, and it's been a good two decades since I last caught a fish. Still I feel it makes a big difference that there's more than just asphalt in every direction. For many people fishing and hunting is one of the biggest reasons they live here. Though the winters seem shorter, the major changes we're experiencing are not to do with climate but tourism. We have many more people visiting each year though if it gets too warm that will be challenging. The thing about Lapland is the snow, the peace and quiet. Besides, if there's no snow, Santa's sledge gets stuck at the runway and that's bad for all the children. Not just the kids in Rovaniemi!'

P187 Left to right: Nala sits out the rain, Kotzebue. 2009; I first met hunter Laurent Kringayark in town, but as soon as we were out on the tundra he came alive. He took me to his hunting shed, before heading further along the coast. Repulse Bay. 2010; Rosalina gives Tara a lift on her snow-mobile, Repulse Bay. 2010.

P188 Clockwise from top left: Working our way round the community in Kotzebue, was a little like being passed from hand to hand. People were so welcoming and friendly and were soon coming forward wanting to meet with us and have their picture taken; Eli Nygård, foot therapist, Træna. 2007; Bus stop at the airport, Rovaniemi. 2006; Returning to St Petersburg, I photograph train hostess Yulia as we pass through the 'Arctic Circle' Polyana Krug station. 2011.

P191 And who so trusteth in the Lord, happy is he. Kotzebue. 2009.

P192 Ginny Alexander runs the small guesthouse in Fort Yukon. 2009. A talented writer, we were delighted when she agreed to share some thoughts on life on the Arctic Circle for our book.

P194 Left to right: Nick Meyer is one of the hard-working chefs aboard *Akademik Ioffe*. Photographed at sea in the Davis Strait, crossing from Baffin Island to the west coast of Greenland. 2013; Anton with his Dalmation dog, Yar-Sale. 2012; Arnold Fedatov, student, Zhigansk. 2013.

P195 Left to right: Nurse Jason Dau and his new plane, Kotzebue. 2009; Book lovers, Greg and Patricia Harding have a library that's well suited to the long winter night in Kotzebue. 2009; Min Kyoung Kim, South Korean potter, Posio. 2013.

P196 Clockwise from top left: Mike Ivalutanar holds one of his small soapstone carvings, which I'm pleased to say is now above my fireplace at home. He stands on the jawbone of a whale, on the shore just outside of town; Emil Johansson, Murjek. 2007; Sveta, reindeer herder, Yamal Peninsula. 2012; Poonye, civil servant, Yar-Sale. 2012.

P199 Oline Enoksen in the window of her home, Itilleq. 2013.

P200-01 'High-rise' modern living in this Greenlandic apartment block, Sisimiut. 2013.

BACK COVER Maria Manninen, fashion student, Rovaniemi. 2013.

BIOGRAPHIES

PHOTOGRAPHER

CRISTIAN BARNETT is a well-respected portrait photographer. For the last twenty years he has been photographing people on his travels around the world. His editorial images have appeared in leading magazines, including *Vogue, Telegraph, Financial Times* and *Country Living* and as an award-winning food photographer he has worked with Michelin-starred chefs across Europe. He began shooting among the people of the Arctic Circle in 2006 and has crossed sea ice, forest and tundra with many indigenous groups, including the Greenlandic Inuit and the Nenet of Siberia. His next project will involve exploring the early history of analogue photography. He lives in England.

EDITOR

HUW LEWIS-JONES is a historian of exploration with a PhD from the University of Cambridge. He travels in the Arctic and Antarctica each year working as a polar guide. Huw was Curator at the Scott Polar Research Institute, Cambridge and the National Maritime Museum, London and is now an award-winning author, who writes and lectures widely about adventure and the visual arts. His books include *Arctic, Polar Portraits, In Search of the South Pole, The Lifeboat, Mountain Heroes* — Adventure Book of the Year at the World ITB Awards in Germany — and *The Conquest of Everest*, which recently won the History Award at the Banff Mountain Festival. He lives in Cornwall.

OUR CONTRIBUTORS

GINNY ALEXANDER is an author who has lived in the forests of the Arctic Circle for over forty years. She moved to Fort Yukon, Alaska in 1968 where she met and married Clarence Alexander and where they raised their five children. Her husband was Grand Chief of the Gwich'in of Alaska and together, over many years, they compiled the *Gwich'in Dictionary*. Ginny has worked in a variety of jobs including teaching, museum administration, and writing a column for the *Fairbanks Daily Newsminer*. Currently she welcomes guests to stay at her home, the Snowdrift Inn. Life continues to be full of surprises under the blue skies of Fort Yukon.

HUGH BRODY is a celebrated writer, anthropologist and filmmaker. His books include *The Peoples Land, Maps and Dreams* and *Living Arctic*. His award-winning reflection on the human condition, *The Other Side of Eden*, was born from years of living and working with the peoples of the Arctic. Hugh has spent a long career devoted to telling the stories and making films that explain and advance the rights of indigenous people. Since 1997, he has worked with the South African San Institute on oral history and land rights in the Southern Kalahari. He is an Associate of the Scott Polar Research Institute and holds the Canada Research Chair in Aboriginal Studies at the University of the Fraser Valley.

ACKNOWLEDGEMENTS

Without the welcome intervention of Huw and Kari at Polarworld in 2008 this project would never have been completed. I am astonished by the generosity they have shown me, encouraging me to continue with *Life on the Line* when I was uncertain about its future. Their guidance and help on subsequent trips in the Arctic was invaluable and their unfailing quest to make this book the best it could be has been my inspiration. And, not to forget, the friendship and fun we've had on our journeys. Thank you folks.

We were all overwhelmed by the support of our friends, and so many strangers, both in the Arctic and further south. A campaign on Kickstarter raised essential funds that enabled us to complete this book and Frederik Paulsen offered timely support too. Our designer Liz House applied her elegant touch, as did Ginny Alexander, whose words come from the forests of Fort Yukon. Finally, thank you to Hugh Brody for writing so beautifully about the Arctic Circle and its people. You are a poet and a gentleman.

There are many other people who have helped us while in the Arctic. In fact this project has relied to a great extent on their kindness. Special thanks should be given to the following: Martin Reftel, my former assistant, who accompanied me on trips to Sweden and Norway. Timo Jaakola and Katri Konttinen were invaluable on my two Finnish journeys. My first trip to Russia's Kola Peninsula was aided by my old friend Lari Nyroos, the wonderfully eccentric Artur Beifuß as well as our enthusiastic local guide Gennady Alexandrov. I'm hugely indebted to Edward Vallance for working with me on the following two Russian trips. He is someone who not only fully understood my aims and succeeded in helping me achieve them but has an understanding and love for Russia which is both admirable and infectious. In Alaska my trip was aided by the kindness and help of Kristen Dau and John and Saima Chase. Irene Lockhorst in Canada was a generous host and thanks to Graham Dickson and Arctic Kingdom for help with flights to Repulse Bay. Immense thanks to Aaron Lawton of One Ocean Expeditions and the crew of the *Akademik Ioffe* for allowing me to hitch with them around Baffin and across to Greenland, on one of the most exciting and rewarding journeys possible in the Arctic. In beautiful Greenland I was ably assisted by local girl Pilunnguaq Bech. Lastly, in Iceland, to Rannveig Vilhjálmsdóttir in Grimsey who introduced me to almost everyone on the island and also to Erlingur Thoroddssen in Raufarhöfn.

Finally, and most importantly, Jackie deserves all my love for her continuous and good-humoured support since I first nervously mooted the idea for *Life on the Line* over dinner in early 2006. She has patiently watched the money for a new kitchen disappear into flights, hotels, assistants, film, processing and scanning. No matter how thrilling it may be to travel in the Arctic, I always look forward to seeing you again when I come home.

OUR KICKSTARTER FAMILY

SPECIAL SUPPORTERS

Alan and Hilary Boyle
Willie Harcourt-Cooze
Tom and Beth Kerridge
Olly Smith
Genevieve Taylor
Marc Venditto

Charles Birnbach
Simon Blakey
Matt Borowick
Richard Brown
Jonathan Craig
Mark Diacono
Paul Dowling
Paul Dunn
Cheryl Fisher
Andrew Greiner
Steven Greenfield
Matthew Grisoni
Cynthia Inions
Joanna Kafarowski
Jürgen Martens
Jacha Potgieter
Heidi Richardson
Christopher Robb
Hal Robinson
Jennifer Scott
Tomas Skopek
Seamus Taaffe

AND THESE LOVELY FOLKS

Sheri Almond
Ashleigh Annereau
Edward Armitage
Teicher Arnaud
Aleksandrov Artyom
Mimi Aye
David Babb
Roy J. Baron
Gitte Barslund
Fiona Beckett
Andy Bell
Kasia Bernas
Carl Bigmore
Andy Black
James Bowden
Hamish Boyle
Mark Brandon
Nicholas Braun
David Breen
Clare S. Brindley
Jeni Ginge Brixey
Charlotte Brøndum
Terence Arthur Brown
Brian Carroll
Ben Casey
Allan Clayton
Natalie Coleman
Matt Collins
Paolo Cunial
Sheila M. Currie
Angela Darwell
Jot Davies

Anna Melland Davis
Carol Devine
Paolo Di Paolantonio
Mark Dodd
Paula Dodd
Chris and Margy Dodd
Matthew Dodwell
Luanne Doner
Susan Dowling
Hillary Downing
Anna Duke
Angus Edmond
Catriona Edwards
Robin Harvey Edwards
Simon Edwards
Matthew Addison Eley
Saeed Taji Farouky
José Angel Fernández
Niki Fford
James Finlay
Stuart Fletcher
Scott Ford
Anna Gazeley
Daisy Gilardini
Kristina Gill
Smith and Gilmore
Robert Grainger
Liz Grec
Jonathan Haber
Miranda Harvey
Sue Herdman
Will Hide
Andy Hinds
Miss Hope

Elin Hopley
Craig Horan
Chris Horwood
Amanda Hudson
Charles Inkin
Matt Inwood
Laurence Jacobson
Leona Jacobson
Michele Jameson
Rikke Bergmann Johansen
Abigail Johnson
Jinny Johnson
Peter Jordan
Paul Joyce
George Julian
Rebecca J. Kaye
Scott Keir
Moki Kokoris
Anna Koska
George Kourounis
Shelina Lalji
David Languignon
Richard Lavanture
Zecca Lehn
Stephan van der Linden
Jean and Jon Lippett
Jostein Liverød
Eric Lloyd
Ross Mackenzie
Emma Marsden
Thomas Matson
Kate McCutcheon
Martin McCutcheon
Scott McIntyre

Nigel Millard
Peter Miller
Anne-Mieke Minderhoud
Nick Miners
Ana-Moly
Carolyn Monastra
Louise Morgan
Ronald J. Moser Jr
Jose Mosquera
Keri Moss
Neil Myers
Natalie Ohlson
Ryan Oliver
Luca Ometto
Billy Palmer
Adomas Paltanavičius
Caroline Parrott
Johnny Patience
Justine Pattison
Old Town Paul
Astrid Piepschyk
Mads Pihl
Anil V. Pillai
Anthony Pilling
Miles Pilling
Matthew Pryor
Michael Reed
Maureen Richmond
Dan Ritzman
Jen and Joe Roberts
Mark Robinson
Denise Rogers
Timothy Rollwagen
Christoph Ruhsam

Chris Rutherford
Jane Scanlan
Lars Schneider
Geoff Shaw
Valentina Sielecki
Adam Simmonds
Søren Skøt
Olna Jenn Smith
Carlton Solle
Eirik Sønneland
Sammy Jo Squir
Rosie Stancer
Joni Sternbach
Dan Stevens
Valeska Stupak
John Summerton
Frederick Swanson
Tamzin Swayne
John Swindell
Melanie Sydow
Ruth Taylor
Philip Tierney
James Turnbull
Penny Turnbull
Rob Tyers
Nathalie Van Meurs
Joël Wagner
Alison Walker
Jo Walker
Becca Watson
Tessa Webb
Chelsea Whyte
Maren Winkler
Tim Young

66° 33' 44" N

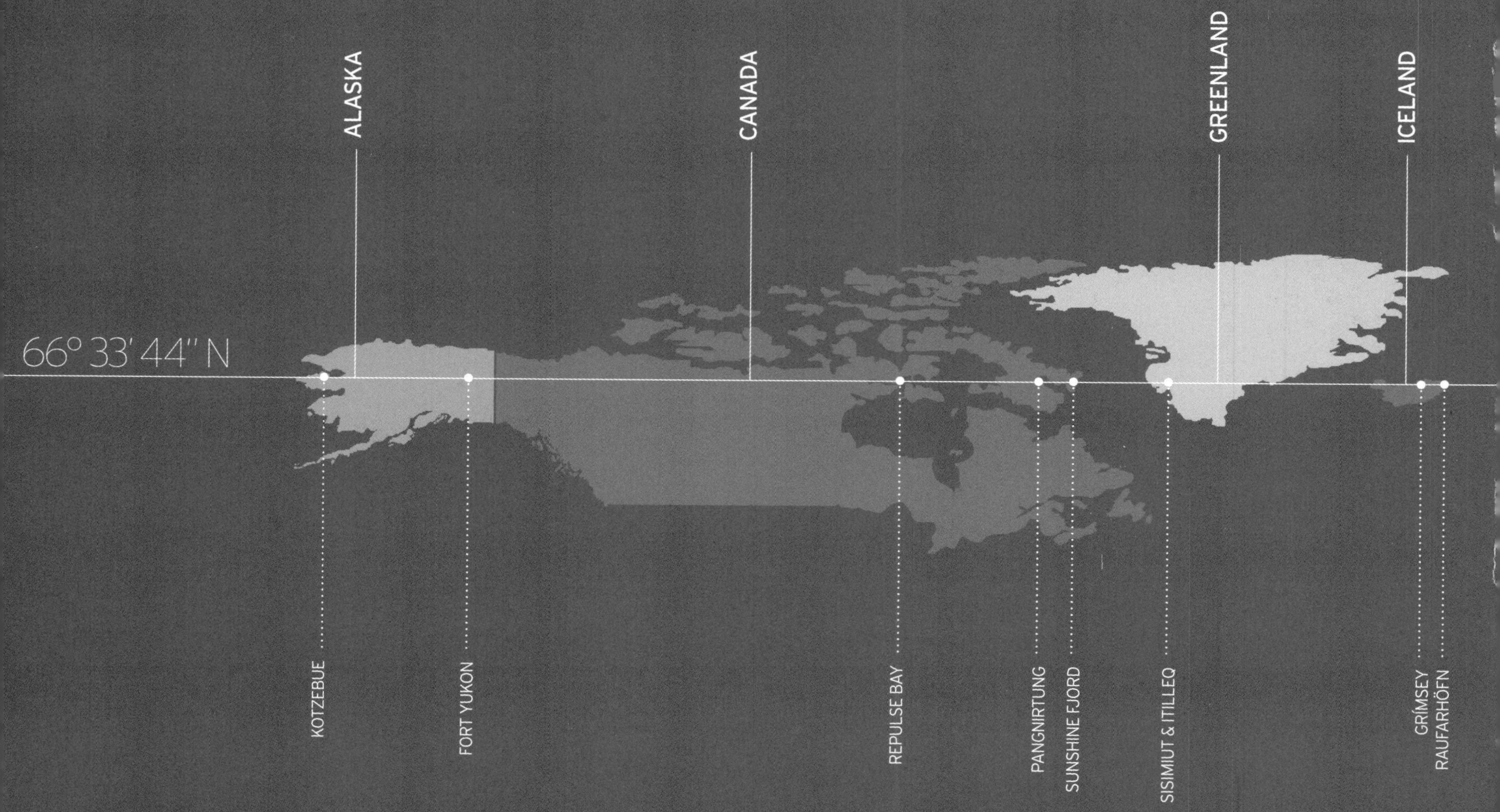
66° 33' 44'' N
ALASKA
CANADA
GREENLAND
ICELAND
KOTZEBUE
FORT YUKON
REPULSE BAY
PANGNIRTUNG
SUNSHINE FJORD
SISIMIUT & ITILLEQ
GRÍMSEY
RAUFARHÖFN